Persevere

This short devotional reminds me of hiding vegetables in stews so that our young son was eating healthily without realizing it. *Persevere* is packed full of essential theology, especially important when the going gets tough. It comes in bite-sized, easy-to-read, inspirational portions, wrapped up in challenging, thought-provoking, helpful and healing passages. There is no 'junk' here. It's all 'food', essential for our walk with God, whatever the terrain.

Catherine Campbell, author of Journey with Me, *IVP, CRT Book of the Year 2019*

I have been truly inspired, fed and encouraged to persevere in my Christian walk with the Lord as I have read again these wonderful passages of Scripture from Psalms to Revelation, with their helpful commentaries.

Maud Kells OBE, missionary and author of An Open Door, *10Publishing*

30-DAY DEVOTIONAL

Persevere

Edited by Elizabeth McQuoid

INTER-VARSITY PRESS
36 Causton Street, London SW1P 4ST, England
Email: ivp@ivpbooks.com
Website: www.ivpbooks.com

First published 2020

British Library Cataloguing-in-Publication Data
A catalogue record for this book is available from the British Library.

ISBN: 978–1–78974–102–5
eBook ISBN: 978–1–78974–103–2

Set in Avenir 11/15pt
Typeset in Great Britain by CRB Associates, Potterhanworth, Lincolnshire
Printed in Great Britain by Ashford Colour Press Ltd, Gosport, Hampshire

Inter-Varsity Press publishes Christian books that are true to the Bible and that communicate the gospel, develop discipleship and strengthen the church for its mission in the world.

IVP originated within the Inter-Varsity Fellowship, now the Universities and Colleges Christian Fellowship, a student movement connecting Christian Unions in universities and colleges throughout Great Britain, and a member movement of the International Fellowship of Evangelical Students. Website: www.uccf.org.uk. That historic association is maintained, and all senior IVP staff and committee members subscribe to the UCCF Basis of Faith.

Contributors

Psalm 130
Nigel Lee
Nigel worked with Operation Mobilisation in India, was Head of Student Ministries for UCCF (University and Colleges Christian Fellowship) and was a consultant in evangelism and Bible teaching for the Whitfield Institute. He was a regular contributor to BBC Radio 4's 'Thought for the Day'.

Ephesians 1:3–23
Rico Tice
Rico is Senior Minister (Evangelism) at All Souls Church, Langham Place in London. He is the co-founder of Christianity Explored Ministries and a speaker at missions and evangelistic events around the world. He is the author of *Honest Evangelism* and *Capturing God.*

1 Thessalonians 3:1–13
Jonathan Lamb
Jonathan is Minister-at-Large for Keswick Ministries. He previously served as CEO of Keswick Ministries and

Director of Langham Preaching. He is the author of a number of books, including *Integrity: Leading with God Watching* and *Preaching Matters: Encountering the Living God.* He also serves as a Vice President of IFES (International Fellowship of Evangelical Students).

2 Timothy 2:1–13 and James 1:1–8
Michael Baughen

Michael served as Rector of Holy Trinity Church in Platt Lane, Rusholme, Manchester, and at All Souls, Langham Place in London, before becoming the Bishop of Chester. Following his retirement, he worked as an honorary assistant bishop in the Diocese of London and in the Diocese of Southwark. He is also a hymn writer.

Hebrews 4:14–16
David Coffey

David was the General Secretary of the Baptist Union of Great Britain. He then became the President of the Baptist World Alliance, and is now the Global Ambassador for BMS World Mission.

Hebrews 6:1–20
Andy Prime

Andy is a graduate of Oak Hill College, London, and was previously Associate Pastor at Charlotte Chapel in

Edinburgh. In September 2014, he joined 20schemes and began a church plant in an Edinburgh scheme (or estate) called Gracemount.

Hebrews 12:1–17
Ivor Poobalan
Ivor is the Principal of the Colombo Theological Seminary (CTS), an evangelical interdenominational seminary in Sri Lanka. He studied at London School of Theology in the UK, Trinity Divinity School in Illinois, USA, and the University of Cape Town, South Africa. He co-chairs the Lausanne Movement's Theology Working Group.

1 Peter 4:12 – 5:14
Matthew Sleeman
Matthew is a lecturer in New Testament and Greek, and chaplain at Oak Hill College. He has written two books for children: *Meet Jesus in Mark* and *Follow Jesus with Peter.* Prior to coming to Oak Hill, Matthew was curate in Eynsham and Cassington, villages near Oxford.

Revelation 22:8–21
Ian Coffey
Ian is a Baptist minister who has led churches in suburban, city-centre and international contexts. He was a member of the leadership team of Spring Harvest for nine years,

and is currently Vice Principal (Strategy) and Director of Leadership Training at Moorlands, a theological training college on the south coast of England.

Preface

What is the collective name for a group of preachers? A troop, a gaggle, a chatter, a pod . . . ? I'm not sure! But in this Food for the Journey series we have gathered an excellent group of Bible teachers to help us unpack the Scriptures and explain some of the core issues that every Christian needs to know and understand.

Each book is based on a particular theme and contains excerpts from messages given by much-loved Keswick Convention speakers, past and present. Where necessary, the language has been updated, but, on the whole, this is what you would have heard had you been listening in the tent on Skiddaw Street. A wide, though not exhaustive, selection of Bible passages explores the key theme, and each day of the devotional ends with a fresh section of application, designed to help you apply God's Word to your own life and situation.

Whether you are a Convention regular or have never been to Keswick, this Food for the Journey series is a unique opportunity to study the Scriptures and particular topics with a range of gifted Bible teachers by your side.

Each book is designed to fit in your jacket pocket, rucksack or handbag, so you can read it anywhere – over the breakfast table, on the commute into work or college, while you are waiting in your car, over your lunch break or in bed at night. Wherever life's journey takes you, time in God's Word is vital nourishment for your spiritual journey.

Our prayer is that these devotionals become your daily feast, a nourishing opportunity to meet with God through his Word. Read, meditate, apply and pray through the Scriptures for each day, and allow God's truths to take root and transform your life.

If these devotionals whet your appetite for more, there is a 'For further study' section at the end of each book. You can also visit our website <www.keswickministries.org> to find the full range of books, study guides, CDs, DVDs and mp3s available.

Let the word of Christ dwell in you richly.
(Colossians 3:16, ESV)

Introduction
Let's die climbing

In the mountains of Switzerland, Amy Carmichael noticed the freshly turned grave of a mountaineer killed in an avalanche. The inscription on the headstone caught her eye. It simply said, 'He died climbing.' The grit and determination of the climber is a captivating picture of Christian service, and an illustration of Amy's own life experience.

Amy sensed God calling her to be a missionary at the Keswick Convention in 1887, but her journey to serve him overseas was fraught with roadblocks. Ill health derailed initial plans to go to China and instead she went to Japan. Unfortunately, illness also resulted in her returning home after only eighteen months. Amy finally made it to India, where she served for fifty-five years. She worked tirelessly to learn the language and culture, and, despite opposition and danger, set out to rescue girls from temple prostitution. She was bedridden for much of her final two decades, but still continued her devotional writing as well as leading the mission's work.

Amy Carmichael's situation was unique, but we too all face struggles, opposition, disappointments and un-answered questions. You would think that with God on our side and the Holy Spirit dwelling in us, we would dance through the raindrops a little more than we do. In some ways, being a Christian makes our struggles harder to bear because we know that we have an all-powerful God who *could* intervene. And yet, more often than not, instead of removing these difficulties, God asks us to persevere, trusting in his sovereignty.

Examples and encouragements for us to persevere and run the Christian race until the very end are laced through-out the Bible. The apostle James reminds us: 'Blessed is the one who perseveres under trial because, having stood the test, that person will receive the crown of life that the Lord has promised to those who love him' (James 1:12).

Paul also urges us to persevere, following his example:

> I press on to take hold of that for which Christ Jesus took hold of me . . . I do not consider myself yet to have taken hold of it. But one thing I do: forgetting what is behind and straining towards what is ahead, I press on towards the goal to win the prize for which God has called me heavenwards in Christ Jesus.
> (Philippians 3:12–14)

Rather than being the exception, perseverance is the norm for Christian living and a sign of our maturity. It is not a character trait we wake up with one morning, but a quality cultivated over many years as, in the midst of opposition, struggles and sorrows, we put our trust in God and daily prove his faithfulness. As we persevere, God refines our faith, teaching us to depend on him and allowing our broken lives more and more to display the glory of the gospel to those around us. Mercifully, this 'long obedience in the same direction' (to use the title of a book by Eugene Peterson, IVP, 2019) is not dependent on us clinging on to God. God preserves his people and holds us fast in the grip of his grace.

This devotional book covers a wide sweep of Scripture passages. Although we can't deal exhaustively with the theme of 'perseverance', the selected passages will build a composite picture of how we can keep going in difficult days. Each passage was written to a group of believers who, no doubt, often felt like giving up. They faced various scenarios, many of which we can identify with: problems in the church, external opposition, concern about the future, even personal struggles with temptation, doubt, guilt and sin. In each case the Bible writers encouraged them, and us, to press on by refocusing on God and on the truths of his Word.

The inscription on that climber's newly planted headstone was the inspiration behind one of Amy's best-known poems:

> Make us Thy mountaineers;
> we would not linger on the lower slope,
> fill us afresh with hope, oh God of Hope,
> that undefeated we may climb the hill
> as seeing Him who is invisible.
>
> Let us die climbing. When this little while
> lies far behind us, and the last defile
> is all alight, and in that light we see
> our Leader and our Lord – what will it be?
> (Amy Carmichael, 'The Last Defile', in *Toward Jerusalem*, Triangle, 1987, p. 85)

Will you die climbing?

Psalms

Imagine being able to sing the songs Jesus sang or pray the prayers he prayed. Well, you can! Jesus, like many Israelites before and after him, used the Psalms in his public and private worship. The Psalms is a collection of prayers and songs, gathered over a number of centuries and written by a variety of authors, including King David. They are full of personal testimony, but direct our focus to God as King and Creator, Judge and Redeemer, Helper and Deliverer. Each psalm is carefully crafted poetry, rich in imagery, and, although written for a specific context, contains timeless truths. On any and every occasion, we can go to the Psalms and find words to express our emotions, words of Scripture we can use to speak to God.

Day 1

Read Psalm 130
Key verses: Psalm 130:1–2

....

> [1] *Out of the depths I cry to you, L*ORD*;*
>   [2] *Lord, hear my voice.*
> *Let your ears be attentive*
>   *to my cry for mercy.*

Are you in the 'depths', full of despair and facing discouragement?

The Bible is honest and acknowledges how we feel. Psalm 130 was written by a man on his way to join the national celebrations in the temple. It is one of a group of psalms from 120 to 134 known as the 'Songs of Ascent' – songs the Jews sang on their pilgrimage to Jerusalem to meet God three times a year. Instead of sharing the excitement of the crowd, this man is crying to God 'out of the depths'.

There could be many reasons for his despair, but here it seems to be a growing consciousness of sin. Every step and every day take him nearer to a God he doesn't really want to face. Maybe it is a sense of national sin, but I suspect that it is more his own guilty conscience about the way he himself has been living. He is coming to an occasion when people gather from all over the country, and he knows he is going to hear the Word of God read and he will have to sing the praises of God. And there are aspects of his own life – selfishness and disobedience – that need to be dealt with before he gets to the end of the journey.

This happens to us too. Sin stops us running, as the psalmist puts it, 'in the way of your commandments' (Psalm 119:32, ESV). It is a great thing to get up in the morning and say, 'I want to run, Lord, in the way of your commands.' But sin hinders and so easily entangles us (Hebrews 12:1). The Lord graciously brings us to these points in our lives where we must face reality and not be anaesthetized any longer to how we have offended and hurt him.

It does not matter what depths of circumstances or sin you are in – cry out to God. He will hear you.

If you are in the depths today because of sin, will you cry out to God for mercy? If you are in the depths today because of hardship or loss, do the single most important thing you can do: cry out to the God who hears.

> It little matters where we are if we can pray; but prayer is never more real and acceptable than when it rises out of the worst places. Deep places beget deep devotion. Depths of earnestness are stirred by depths of tribulation. Diamonds sparkle most amid the darkness. He that prays in the depth will not sink out of his depth.
> (C. H. Spurgeon, *Psalms, Vol. 1*, Crossway Classic Commentary, Crossway, 1994, p. 281)

Day 2

Read Psalm 130
Key verses: Psalm 130:3–4

....

> ³*If you, LORD, kept a record of sins,*
> *Lord, who could stand?*
> ⁴*But with you there is forgiveness,*
> *so that we can, with reverence, serve you.*

Is your heart feeling cold towards God? Have you lost the joy of serving him?

According to Psalm 130:4, the remedy we need is personal forgiveness. There is no law, no set of rules, no guilt trip that could motivate us to keep on living to please God. The only thing that makes our hearts run after the Lord Jesus is receiving God's forgiveness and appreciating his sheer grace and mercy towards us.

No one in the history of the world has ever come to God in heartfelt repentance and not received forgiveness. That was what the Old Testament declared in Exodus

34:6–7: 'The LORD, the LORD, the compassionate and gracious God, slow to anger, abounding in love and faithfulness, maintaining love to thousands, and forgiving wickedness, rebellion and sin.'

With me, sin; with the Lord, forgiveness. You may have grasped this wonderful truth and lived in the light of it for years; it's the anchor of your life. Or you may be aware of the stain of sin in your heart and wonder how you can possibly keep calling yourself a Christian. Do you know that you could write down everything about yourself that is an offence to God, and your friends and even the angel Gabriel could add to the list, but Christ forgives all your sins and doesn't keep the record?

If he doesn't keep the record, what does he keep in heaven? He keeps his wounds: 'Rich wounds, yet visible above, in beauty glorified' (Matthew Bridges, 'Crown Him with Many Crowns', 1852). And Jesus knows why his wounds are there: they are there so that you and I can be there. In heaven, Jesus has not forgotten that you and I are sinners, but rather he chooses not to keep the record. He will not hold our sins against us. Instead, we experience the kindness of God demonstrated at Calvary. Such extravagant forgiveness, such grace, melts our indifference and compels us to love and serve God with grateful hearts.

Mediate on the full and final forgiveness for sin that Christ achieved on the cross.

> When you were dead in your sins and in the un-circumcision of your flesh, God made you alive with Christ. He forgave us all our sins, having cancelled the charge of our legal indebtedness, which stood against us and condemned us; he has taken it away, nailing it to the cross. And having disarmed the powers and author-ities, he made a public spectacle of them, triumphing over them by the cross.
> (Colossians 2:13–15)

Today, in view of this forgiveness, press on in loving and serving God.

Day 3

Read Psalm 130
Key verses: Psalm 130:5–8

....

⁵I wait for the Lᴏʀᴅ, my whole being waits,
and in his word I put my hope.
⁶I wait for the Lord
more than watchmen wait for the morning,
more than watchmen wait for the morning.

⁷Israel, put your hope in the Lᴏʀᴅ,
for with the Lᴏʀᴅ is unfailing love
and with him is full redemption.
⁸He himself will redeem Israel
from all their sins.

In general, we don't like waiting. It seems a waste of time, as well as an acknowledgment that we are not in control. But the waiting of the psalmist in Psalm 130 is not like the anxious waiting for test results from the hospital or the futile waiting in a traffic jam. It is completely different. It is eager and active; the psalmist is preparing himself to meet God.

The psalmist has decided, 'Whatever my circumstances, whatever's happening, I will wait for the Lord.' Notice that it's personal. He's not waiting for correct doctrine or a good meeting; he's not even waiting for forgiveness; he is waiting for the Lord. His soul is engaged; the innermost core of his being is going to wait for his coming. He is waiting for God's ultimate coming when the heavens are going to be unzipped and the Lord will appear with the angels. But he is also waiting for those other occasions when we meet God, the kind the Lord talked about in John 14:21: 'Whoever has my commands and keeps them is the one who loves me. The one who loves me will be loved by my Father, and I too will love them and show myself to them.'

'I am going to wait,' says the psalmist, 'for those manifestations of the Lord to my own soul. I am going to wait more than watchmen wait for the morning.' The watchmen would stand on the ramparts waiting for morning light. They knew the sunrise would come, so they waited with hopeful, trusting, patient expectation. So it is with that kind of hope that the psalmist waits.

Can you see how the psalm develops? The psalmist started off in the depths and then he began to pray. He found relief in God's unconditional forgiveness, began to hope that the Lord would visit him, and then his hope grew to expectancy because of the Lord's character – his unfailing love and full redemption (verse 7).

Likewise, we can wait on God because we know his character. We know and have experienced his forgiveness and unfailing love. We can also trust in God's Word. We have seen him keep his promises, not least in the full redemption he offers us in the Lord Jesus.

Are you, like the psalmist, putting your hope in God's Word and his character? Isaiah 26:8 teaches us how to wait well:

Yes, LORD, walking in the way of your laws,
we wait for you;
your name and renown
are the desire of our hearts.

Ephesians, 1 Thessalonians, 2 Timothy

God changes lives. The apostle Paul is probably the best-known example of God's transforming power. This former persecutor of Christians became a passionate evangelist, sharing the gospel and establishing churches in various cities. The majority of the New Testament letters are written by him to individual believers and to these new churches, urging them to press on in the faith.

Ephesians

God's high calling for the church is the resounding theme of Ephesians. Paul had stayed in Ephesus for three years, planting a church. This commercial centre was a strategic place for evangelism from which the gospel spread to the surrounding communities. No doubt Paul's letter was intended to be circulated to all the churches in the area. Unusually, Paul is not addressing a particular error or heresy, but writing to remind believers that the church displays God's 'manifold wisdom' (Ephesians 3:10) and so they should serve one another, seeking unity and maturity.

1 Thessalonians

The book of 1 Thessalonians is essentially a follow-up letter to new Christians. Persecution forced Paul and his companions to flee the busy seaport city of Thessalonica sooner than he would have wished, leaving a group of very new Jew and Gentile converts (Acts 17:1–10). Paul wrote to these believers from Corinth, encouraging them to stand firm in persecution and providing the instruction he had hoped to give in person. A major theme in this letter is the second coming of Christ.

2 Timothy

This letter records Paul's last words. He is in prison, chained to a Roman soldier, dictating this letter to Luke for his young pastor friend, Timothy, Paul's 'true son in the faith' (1 Timothy 1:2). Timothy had been his travelling companion on missionary journeys, had visited churches on his behalf, was with him during his first stint in prison and was now the pastor of the church in Ephesus. Paul wrote to Timothy encouraging him to visit, but, more importantly, pleading with him to keep Christ and the gospel central to his life and ministry.

Day 4

Read Ephesians 1:3–23
Key verses: Ephesians 1:15–16

∙∙∙

15For this reason, ever since I heard about your faith in the Lord Jesus and your love for all God's people, 16I have not stopped giving thanks for you, remembering you in my prayers.

When you consider your church, what thoughts spring to mind? In Ephesians 1, Paul is reflecting on a congregation. And his reflection excites and overwhelms him so much that he falls into both prayer and praise. Why? Because, in that congregation, he sees what God has done behind the scenes of history.

So think of your church. It is there you meet because God has been at work since the beginning of time. He chose you before the beginning of time (verse 4). He sent Jesus to die for you (verse 7). Despite the immense barriers of race, class, culture, intellect and age, amazingly he's made you into a family (verse 13). And the Spirit was given to turn our hearts around when we were fully against him, which is no small thing (verse 14). One day, you'll stand before God and he'll say, 'It's good to see you. You've been on my mind a very long time.'

Do you think about the members of your church like that? Do you appreciate the value God has placed on them? If we're not thinking this about our own churches, then the devil's got hold of our thinking and resentment can come flooding through. You may have been hurt by painful experiences that have happened at church. You may be scraping around for self-esteem because there have been lies told about you and some horrible things have happened. That's why people who are committed Christians, or so-called Christians, just walk away from church.

But in these verses, Paul tells us how we can stay and persevere through the hard times in church life. You take the horrible things that have been said and you apply Ephesians 1. When it comes to church, the great aim of the devil is to cause resentment to grow in your heart. If you're constantly looking for problems in church life, you'll find them, and you'll become bitter. Instead, meditate on Ephesians 1 and all that God has done in, for and through the church. Reflect on God's love for the church, and let that shape how you think, feel and act towards your brothers and sisters in Christ.

How did Paul keep on loving the church? The key is thankfulness. He reflected on all that God had done for these believers in Christ and the value God had placed on them, and he couldn't help being thankful (verse 16). Will you try being more thankful? Perhaps every morning and night, kneel and give thanks to God. Why don't you start by thanking God for your church family and what Christ did for them? Watch how this one spiritual habit transforms your feelings and causes you to make very different choices.

Day 5

Read 1 Thessalonians 3:1–13
Key verses: 1 Thessalonians 3:2–5

• •

2We sent Timothy . . . to strengthen and encourage you in your faith, 3so that no one would be unsettled by these trials. For you know quite well that we are destined for them. 4In fact, when we were with you, we kept telling you that we would be persecuted. And it turned out that way, as you well know. 5For this reason, when I could stand it no longer, I sent to find out about your faith. I was afraid that in some way the tempter had tempted you and that our labours might have been in vain.

How can we resist the temptations offered by our secular society? How can we keep living for Jesus in a pluralistic context where he is denied?

The church in Thessalonica was facing all kinds of pressures. Paul had only been there for three weeks. What chance would such a church have of being established, let alone maturing? But notice verse 8: 'For now we really live, since you are standing firm in the Lord.' These believers were rock solid! How? They were 'standing firm *in the Lord*'. They sustained their steadfast commitment by being in close union with the Lord. He was the rock on which they stood, the one who strengthened their resolve to live with faith and love.

Paul wanted these young believers, and us, to know that the trials that threaten to unsettle our faith (verse 3) and the temptations of Satan (verse 5) are inevitable. It is not just a matter of chance or blind fate: the emphasis of verse 3 is that this is something within God's purpose. You are destined or appointed for these trials. Mysterious as it might seem, God's hand is in such trials, and he will use them for his particular purposes.

Whatever the source of the hardships, we can hold on to the truth that we are never beyond God's sovereign care; the situation is never out of control. We can hold on to the rock-solid certainties of God's good purposes and fatherly care. Pressures are part of living out the Christian life, and, if we allow them to, can strengthen our commitment to stand firm in the Lord.

In the trials and hardships you face, will you 'stand firm', trusting that God is in control and working out his good purposes? Will you seek to let these circumstances refine your faith and mould you into the character of Christ?

John Bunyan, the author of *The Pilgrim's Progress*, wisely (and quaintly) explained the value of trying days in the following:

> We are apt to overshoot, in the days that are calm, and to think ourselves far higher, and more strong than we find we be when the trying day is upon us . . . We could not live without such turnings of the hand of God upon us. We should be overgrown with flesh, if we had not our seasonable winters.
>
> (John Bunyan, *Seasonable Counsel*, CreateSpace Independent Publishing, 2014, p. 4)

Day 6

Read 1 Thessalonians 3:1–13
Key verse: 1 Thessalonians 3:2

....

²We sent Timothy, who is our brother and co-worker in God's service in spreading the gospel of Christ, to strengthen and encourage you in your faith.

What do you talk about when you get together with Christian friends? Sport, the weather, church politics? What about making it your aim to encourage one another to persevere in the faith?

That is why Paul sent Timothy to Thessalonica. Paul was in Athens, about to face the philosophers and idolaters and perhaps another hostile reaction. But he writes, 'When we could stand it no longer, we thought it best to be *left* by ourselves' (verse 1, emphasis added). The Greek word translated 'left' is a strong word which can be used of being abandoned or even of dying. Paul's concern for his friends was such that he would send one of his closest friends and fellow workers – the very person who could have supported him in a new and challenging mission. What mattered most was the well-being of the small church in Thessalonica.

Look how he describes Timothy's ministry in verse 2: 'We sent Timothy . . . to strengthen and encourage you in your faith.' 'Strengthen' is a word from the building trade; it means to 'buttress'. Timothy's job was to build them up. This strengthening and nurturing is needed both by young Christians who are facing many new challenges and by older Christians who are in danger of becoming spiritually stagnant. He was also to 'encourage', exhorting and urging them to hold on to the apostolic teaching.

More than that, we see in verse 10 that, although they were standing firm, growing in faith and love, there was more to be done. Paul wanted to get back to see them again 'and supply what is lacking in your faith'. Here Paul uses a word that is used of mending nets in Mark 1 and of equipping Christians for the work of ministry in Ephesians 4. He wanted to make good the deficiencies, to restore and equip them for full maturity.

Both Paul's generosity and Timothy's ministry are an example of how to care for those who are under pressure and encourage them to stand firm. In fact, in verse 8, when Paul heard how well the believers were doing, he said, 'Now we really live.' In other words, his life was completely bound up with theirs. That is what Christian fellowship is all about. I feel the pressures that others are facing. And, under pressure myself, I need the encouragement of others who will remind me of God's promises, provoke my faith in the Lord and stand alongside me in the trials.

Remember Barnabas? 'When he arrived [at Antioch] and saw what the grace of God had done, he was glad and encouraged them all to remain true to the Lord with all their hearts' (Acts 11:23). Will you be like Barnabas? One who strengthens and encourages your friends, who urges them to hold on to the truths of the gospel, who reminds them they are not beyond the Spirit's comforting presence or the Father's compassionate care?

Day 7

Read 1 Thessalonians 3:1–13
Key verses: 1 Thessalonians 3:10–13

· ·

[10]*Night and day we pray most earnestly that we may see you again and supply what is lacking in your faith.*

[11]*Now may our God and Father himself and our Lord Jesus clear the way for us to come to you.* [12]*May the Lord make your love increase and overflow for each other and for everyone else, just as ours does for you.* [13]*May he strengthen your hearts so that you will be blameless and holy in the presence of our God and Father when our Lord Jesus comes with all his holy ones.*

A close friend is having a serious operation, or your child is in the middle of an important exam, and you are waiting for news of how it has gone. Every few minutes, it surfaces in your mind again, and you pray. You are so concerned about his or her situation and welfare that it naturally springs to mind.

That's exactly how it should be as we pray for one another. Paul expresses his affectionate concern and remarkable solidarity with these believers in prayer (verse 10). Christians under pressure need us to bring their situations to God. Prayer is deflecting all of our situations God-wards. I like the illustration that the preacher and Bible scholar Alec Motyer used: Christians are like mirrors, angled so that whatever meets us on our journey, we immediately deflect it to God, sending it up to our heavenly Father. Such praying helps us see our problems in proper perspective.

And notice how God-centred Paul's prayer is. Verses 10–13 are full of God's work, heralding what he can do. Think about our prayer meetings. Many of the prayers are: 'O Lord, we ask for . . .', but the great Bible prayers are different. They are not: 'O Lord, we . . .' but 'O Lord, you . . .' Do you remember the prayer of the early Christians in Acts 4, when the small church was under pressure? How did they pray? 'Sovereign Lord . . . you made the heavens and the earth and the sea, and everything in them' (Acts 4:24).

Do you sometimes feel overwhelmed trying to live the Christian life? Do you feel it's impossible to overcome the pull of sin, or to live with integrity in your home or workplace when everyone else has different priorities? Do the problems at church or in your relationships seem beyond your control? Pray for God's mighty power. In Ephesians 1:19–20, Paul describes God's power at work in Jesus' resurrection: 'That power is the same as the mighty strength he exerted when he raised Christ from the dead.' God's power which overcomes death, which elevated Jesus far above all rule and authority, is the same power which is at work in us. It is the resource we need and for which we must pray.

In Ephesians 6:10, Paul urges us: 'Be strong in the Lord and in his mighty power.' Perhaps it would be better to say not 'be strong' but 'be strengthened': receive God's strength, and then you will be strong. Today, pray for yourself and those you know who are struggling. Pray that you would trust in God; that in his strength, you would persevere and live for him.

Day 8

Read 1 Thessalonians 3:1–13
Key verses: 1 Thessalonians 3:11–13

....

[11] Now may our God and Father himself and our Lord Jesus clear the way for us to come to you. [12] May the Lord make your love increase and overflow for each other and for everyone else, just as ours does for you. [13] May he strengthen your hearts so that you will be blameless and holy in the presence of our God and Father when our Lord Jesus comes with all his holy ones.

In many parts of the world, Christians are in the minority, sometimes living under oppressive governments. Even in our increasingly secular culture, it is easy for believers to feel vulnerable. To stand firm and stay strong, we need to recover our conviction that God is unstoppable, that he will complete the work which he began. Paul's prayer reminds us:

- God directs (verse 11).

  Paul prayed for God to make it possible for him to visit the Thessalonians, and God answered his prayers. Paul was able to visit them on his way back to Jerusalem. Satan might hinder, but ultimately God's purposes are unstoppable.

- God equips (verse 12).

  Our spiritual growth is in God's hands. But this is a partnership. So, on the one hand, Paul sees it as God's work: 'May the Lord make your love increase' (verse 12). But on the other hand, in the next chapter, he says, 'You do love all of God's family . . . we urge you . . . to do so more and more' (4:10). There is a God-centredness, but that stimulates, not lessens, our sense of responsibility. We cooperate with God to activate his purposes in our lives.

- God completes (verse 13).

  God will complete the work which he has begun in our lives. 'Blameless' implies unblameable. On that future day when Jesus returns, nothing will stand against us; Satan's accusations cannot harm us. Surely there's no greater encouragement to live the life of faith – to live in holiness, to stand firm – than the prospect of Christ's return. Fixing our eyes on Jesus, the coming King, sets all of our trials and satanic pressures in perspective.

God helps us stand firm and persevere. However, ultimately it is not our hold of God that matters, but his hold of us:

> The eternal God is your refuge,
> and underneath are the everlasting arms.
> (Deuteronomy 33:27)

In John 10:27–29, Jesus promises,

> My sheep listen to my voice; I know them, and they follow me. I give them eternal life, and they shall never perish; no one will snatch them out of my hand. My Father, who has given them to me, is greater than all; no one can snatch them out of my Father's hand.

Today, rejoice that, despite your present struggles, your eternal salvation is secure. You are held in the grip of God the Father and God the Son. There is no safer place to be.

Day 9

Read 2 Timothy 2:1–13
Key verses: 2 Timothy 2:8–10

....

8 Remember Jesus Christ, raised from the dead, descended from David. This is my gospel, 9 for which I am suffering even to the point of being chained like a criminal. But God's word is not chained. 10 Therefore I endure everything for the sake of the elect, that they too may obtain the salvation that is in Christ Jesus, with eternal glory.

How can we cope when we face crises in our personal lives?

The apostle Paul was dying, and young, diffident Timothy found himself having to step into his mentor's shoes. Paul's encouragement in this trying circumstance was: 'Be strong in the grace that is in Christ Jesus.' He urged Timothy to press on with the commitment of a soldier and the determination of an athlete, and to work hard like a farmer. In a word, he was to endure.

Paul knew all about endurance. He himself was suffering for the gospel, wearing chains like a criminal, yet enduring that suffering and despising the shame for the sake of Christ (verse 9). Indeed, he put endurance top of the list when he wrote that great catalogue of ways to serve the Lord in 2 Corinthians 6:4.

But endurance was not just Paul's idea; it is one of the key words in the New Testament. The apostles Peter, James and John knew it in the context of persecution (1 Peter 2:20; James 5:11). In fact, at the same time as this epistle was being written, John was calling for the endurance of the saints, 'those who keep God's commands and hold fast their testimony about Jesus' (Revelation 12:17). John knew how persecution sought out the Christians who were strong in Christ, and those who were not.

Why does Paul say, 'Remember Jesus Christ' (verse 8)? Because Jesus calls us to endure. Listen to his words in Matthew 10:22: 'You will be hated by everyone because of me, but the one who stands firm to the end will be saved.' We also remember Jesus because he is our example and inspiration:

> let us run with perseverance the race marked out for us, fixing our eyes on Jesus, the pioneer and perfecter of faith. For the joy that was set before him he endured the

cross, scorning its shame, and sat down at the right hand of the throne of God.
(Hebrews 12:1–2)

Paul would not have suffered if he had not believed that the gospel was supremely worth the cost. Endurance is one of the qualities God wants. He wants every Christian to draw on the grace of Christ, to be committed, determined, working hard and ready to endure anything for the sake of the gospel and the Word of God that can never be chained.

It is easy to feel overwhelmed when we focus on our troubles. Today, lift up your eyes and fix them on Jesus rather than on your circumstances. 'Remember Jesus Christ', your:

- Creator (John 1:3)
- Saviour (John 3:16–18)
- Intercessor (Romans 8:34)
- Rescuer (Colossians 1:13)
- Comfort (2 Corinthians 1:3–4)
- Strength (Psalm 28:7)
- Sustainer (Isaiah 46:4)
- Guide (Psalm 139:9–10)

Hebrews

We don't know who wrote the book of Hebrews, but we do know why it was written. In the face of persecution, some Jewish Christians were drifting away from the gospel. Unbelief had crept in, they were not making spiritual progress and they had given up meeting together. Like the earlier generation of Israelites in the desert, they were in danger of facing God's judgment. The writer makes it clear that slipping back into the comfortable ways of Judaism was not an option because Christ's coming had changed the spiritual landscape for ever. Christ was God's full and final revelation; he completed Israel's history, law, ceremonial rituals and priesthood. This book urges believers to persevere in the faith by pointing them to Christ's absolute supremacy in divine revelation and his absolute sufficiency in Christian experience: 'fix your thoughts . . . [and fix your] eyes on Jesus' (Hebrews 3:1; 12:2).

Day 10

Read Hebrews 4:14–16
Key verse: Hebrews 4:14

....

14 Therefore, since we have a great high priest who has ascended into heaven, Jesus the Son of God, let us hold firmly to the faith we profess.

Disobedience, unbelief and hard hearts characterized the Israelites who wandered in the wilderness. The writer to the Hebrews urges us to learn from their mistakes and press on in wholehearted faith.

Look at the bookends that stand on either side of this section of Hebrews 4:14–16. The first is verse 13: 'Nothing in all creation is hidden from God's sight. Everything is uncovered and laid bare before the eyes of him to whom we must give account.' It is a warning. All the verses preceding this are a warning to take God's Word seriously. Why? Because to be exposed to the Word of God is to be exposed to God himself. The language used is that of nakedness. Everything is laid bare. The other bookend is 4:16: 'Let us then approach God's throne of grace with confidence, so that' – having been exposed and found wretched by God's Word – 'we may receive mercy and find grace to help us in our time of need.'

In moments of wretchedness, when God's Word has exposed our sin and guilt, we need to remember verse 14: 'we have a great high priest'. The writer emphasizes this as a present reality, not wishful thinking. He is not hoping it might happen; he is talking about that conscious possession of believers. We possess Jesus! We have this 'great high priest . . . Jesus the Son of God'. Notice the power behind these twin titles: Christ as fully man and fully God, Christ in his humiliation and exaltation, Christ in his sympathy and in his power and glory.

In Hebrews 1:2–3, we learn more about him: he is God's Son, heir of all things, maker and sustainer of the universe, the radiance of God's glory, God himself and an authentic representation of God the Father, our redeemer who has completed the work of redemption and is now ruling with God. No wonder the writer is inspired and wanting to inspire our hearts about what we possess. We possess Jesus, this great high priest.

Thank God that we possess Jesus, this great high priest, now. This means that the sacrifice he made once and for all is effectual *now*; if you confess your sins, he forgives you *now*; he is interceding for you *now*; he makes the way to the Father open *now*. In the light of this, and in the power of the Holy Spirit, 'hold firmly to the faith [you] profess'. Don't let doubt, disbelief or guilt throw you off course.

No condemnation now I dread;
Jesus, and all in Him is mine!
Alive in Him, my living Head,
and clothed in righteousness divine,
bold I approach th'eternal throne,
and claim the crown, through Christ my own.
(Charles Wesley, 'And Can It Be', 1738)

Day 11

Read Hebrews 4:14–16
Key verse: Hebrews 4:14

....

14 Therefore, since we have a great high priest who has ascended into heaven, Jesus the Son of God, let us hold firmly to the faith we profess.

Red tape, protocols, months of planning and vetting are required for anyone meeting the royal family today. By contrast, we have permanent access to the King of kings. This is an amazing privilege.

How is such access possible? Because Jesus, our great high priest, has 'ascended into heaven'. We need to turn to the Old Testament for some context. Once a year, the high priest was allowed to enter the holy of holies through the temple curtain, beyond the eyes of the people, to atone for the sins of the nation. And on the day that Jesus died that temple curtain was torn from top to bottom (Matthew 27:51). The way to God's presence is now permanently open. In Hebrews 9:24, the writer explains that

Christ did not enter a man-made sanctuary like the priests who had gone before. He entered heaven itself, and now he appears on our behalf in God's presence. That's what makes him a great high priest.

And when he talks about ascending into heaven, he is not giving you a cosmic geography lesson. He doesn't even want you to ponder where heaven might be. What he is really saying is that the one who ascended is the one who transcended all limits of time and space, so that, in accordance with Scripture, he is made higher than the heavens. And he has ascended far above all the heavens so that he might fulfil all things in that place of rule and authority, where the fight is over, the battle won and the victory secure.

Our great high priest has secured for us permanent access to God the Father because he passed through the heavens as the transcended Lord. The same Jesus who was born at Bethlehem, walked in Palestine, died on Calvary, rose in Jerusalem, ascended from earth and is now crowned with glory and honour is the great high priest who now appears on our behalf in God's presence.

It doesn't matter whether it is day or night, whether you have been obedient or have fallen into sin again, whether you are joyful or weighed down with cares –

you have access to God. By his blood shed on the cross and his mighty resurrection to glory, Jesus has for ever opened the way to the Father. God wants you to come into his presence. Being with him – reading and meditating on his Word and praying – is vital if we are to persevere in our faith journey. He invites you today to come to him for forgiveness, strengthening, refreshment and comfort. The way is open; it is up to you to take the next step (Revelation 3:20).

> Come near to God and he will come near to you. Wash your hands, you sinners, and purify your hearts, you double-minded.
> (James 4:8)

Day 12

Read Hebrews 4:14–16
Key verse: Hebrews 4:15

....

> ¹⁵*For we do not have a high priest who is unable to feel sympathy for our weaknesses, but we have one who has been tempted in every way, just as we are – yet he did not sin.*

What is your greatest temptation? Where are you vulnerable? What are the weak spots the devil targets again and again?

We are probably more secretive about our temptations than about any other aspect of Christian living, but Jesus knows all about them.

Verse 15 may be misunderstood in two ways. First, the verse does not say Jesus encountered every conceivable temptation. For example, he could not have experienced the temptations of those over forty, a married couple or a single woman. Second, this verse does not concede that if Jesus could be tempted and yet was incapable of sinning, his temptation in the wilderness, and in other aspects of his ministry, was nothing more than a charade. That is a ploy of the enemy to destroy your confidence in your great high priest. It is unthinkable that Jesus should have succumbed to that temptation that leads to sin, but never, ever, minimize the reality of the confrontation between Jesus and the tempter.

God restrains the power of temptation in the believer's life so we are not tempted beyond what we can bear; there is a way out. The temptation we meet is filtered through God's protecting hand: that's the way out. In Jesus' case, the filter was removed. His temptations were real: the forty days of unbroken temptation in the wilderness, where Satan offered him alternative routes to the kingdom (Matthew 4); the moment Satan tempted him through Peter, who refused to believe Jesus had to go to Jerusalem to die (Matthew 16:21–23); when he was tempted in the garden of Gethsemane to avoid the suffering ahead (Matthew 26:39); and his last hours on the cross and the temptation implicit in the invitation: 'Come down from the cross, if you are the Son of God!' (Matthew 27:40).

Have you grasped what happened at Gethsemane? Our Saviour was praying with 'loud cries and tears'

(Hebrews 5:7, ESV). Never doubt his close identity with those who are being tempted. We give in before temptation is fully spent in our bodies. Only the one who doesn't yield knows its full extent. What a great high priest we possess!

Jesus knows what it means to be tempted, and yet he never gave in. His determination to obey his Father overwhelmed his desire to succumb to temptation. Today, draw on his example and strength. As you encounter opportunities to sin, to give up, to be mediocre rather than wholehearted in your obedience, use Jesus' words as your fresh commitment to God: 'Yet not as I will, but as you will' (Matthew 26:39).

Day 13

Read Hebrews 4:14–16
Key verse: Hebrews 4:15

....

¹⁵For we do not have a high priest who is unable to feel sympathy for our weaknesses, but we have one who has been tempted in every way, just as we are – yet he did not sin.

Can Jesus – seated at the right hand of God in heaven, reigning in power and authority – really be a friend of sinners (Hebrews 1:3; Matthew 11:19)?

For those who doubt, the writer to the Hebrews uses explicit language to affirm we have a high priest who has gentle sympathy with our weakness. In his description in Hebrews 5:2, the writer describes the human tradition in which this great priest stands: 'He is able to deal gently with ignorant and wayward people because he himself is subject to the same weaknesses' (NLT). If a human priest is able to deal gently with those who are ignorant and are going astray, how much more so this great high priest?

Jesus' sufferings on earth have produced such sympathy in him that he has never forgotten them: the friends who forsook him in his hour of need (Matthew 26:40); the family who thought he was mad (Mark 3:21); the followers who deserted him, saying, 'We can't cope with teaching like that' (see John 6:66).

Jesus has gentle sympathy with those who are ignorant of the way and those who are ignoring the way. My experience through the years suggests that more Christians are tempted to despair, and even quit, because of the disappointments of life. This can be greater than almost any other temptation that besets us. And disappointment with your circumstances, if not curbed and dealt with, often leads to disappointment in the Lord himself. Don't be alarmed or ashamed if that is how you feel. You are coming to a high priest who is gently sympathetic to all conditions.

Are you disappointed with how your life has turned out? Are you disappointed with God? Don't despair; don't deviate from God's way. Rather, 'hold firmly to the faith [you] profess' (Hebrews 4:14). Come to Jesus, the great high priest and friend of sinners. Speak honestly to him, receive his comfort, listen to his Word.

What a friend we have in Jesus,
all our sins and griefs to bear!
What a privilege to carry
everything to God in prayer!
O what peace we often forfeit,
O what needless pain we bear,
all because we do not carry
everything to God in prayer!

Have we trials and temptations?
Is there trouble anywhere?
We should never be discouraged;
take it to the Lord in prayer!
Can we find a friend so faithful
who will all our sorrows share?
Jesus knows our every weakness;
take it to the Lord in prayer!

Are we weak and heavy laden,
cumbered with a load of care?
Precious Saviour, still our refuge –
take it to the Lord in prayer!
Do your friends despise, forsake you?
Take it to the Lord in prayer!
In his arms he'll take and shield you;
you will find a solace there.
(Joseph Medlicott Scriven, 'What a Friend We Have
in Jesus', 1855)

Day 14

Read Hebrews 4:14–16
Key verse: Hebrews 4:16

....

16Let us then approach God's throne of grace with confidence, so that we may receive mercy and find grace to help us in our time of need.

You may say, 'Who can cope with my misery, failure and despair?' God responds by saying, 'Come to the throne of grace and pour out to me all your needs.'

The way to read verse 16 is: 'Let us keep on approaching, again and again.' And we can come to this throne with 'confidence'. This indicates bold frankness, open, free speech. When the Bible writers use this word, it means, 'Come to the throne of grace and speak about everything; be unembarrassed, unrestricted; pour out your heart.'

I love the way that whenever people heard that Jesus was in a house or street, they approached him boldly. Jairus implored Jesus to help him because his twelve-year-old daughter was dying (Mark 5:22–24). The woman pushed her way through the crowds because she was haemorrhaging and no doctor could help her (Luke 8:43–48). This is boldly approaching the place of grace.

The writer to the Hebrews urges us to 'approach God's throne' to 'receive mercy and find grace to help us in our time of need'. Mercy to cover the sins of yesterday and grace to meet the needs of today. Remember the prodigal son, clutching his spiritual rags around him in his wretchedness and need (Luke 15:11–32)? He was weak, friendless, far from home. All he could do was cast himself upon the father's mercy, and he received a welcoming embrace. But it went beyond that. Here it says that we *receive* mercy and – to our surprise – we *find* grace. Grace is the unexpected blessing. All the prodigal asked for was that he might be able to find mercy. 'What shall I say to my father? "I have sinned, I am no longer worthy to be called your son. I just want to be in the house, in the servants' quarters – just let me come home."' He received mercy, and he *found* grace in the ring, the robe, the shoes, the banquet and the blessing he never deserved and certainly never expected.

Are you in need? Why don't you come to the throne of grace?

Grace goes beyond mercy. Mercy gave the prodigal son a second chance. Grace threw him a party . . . Mercy forgave the thief on the cross. Grace escorted him into paradise. Mercy pardons us. Grace woos and weds us . . . Saving grace saves us from our sins. Sustaining grace . . . surprises us in the middle of our difficulties with ample resources of faith. [It] does not promise the absence of struggle but the presence of God. And according to Paul, God has sufficient sustaining grace to meet every single challenge of our lives . . . *Grace* is simply another word for his tumbling, rumbling reservoir of strength and protection. It comes at us not occasionally or miserly, but constantly and aggressively, wave upon wave.

(Max Lucado, 'Grace: More Than We Deserve, Greater Than We Imagine', *Christianity Today*, 7 May 2013, <https://www.christianitytoday.com/biblestudies/articles/spiritualformation/grace-more-than-we-deserve-greater-than-we-imagine.html>)

Day 15

Read Hebrews 6:1–20
Key verses: Hebrews 6:7–8

....

⁷Land that drinks in the rain often falling on it and that produces a crop useful to those for whom it is farmed receives the blessing of God. ⁸But land that produces thorns and thistles is worthless and is in danger of being cursed. In the end it will be burned.

What evidence is there that you are a Christian? Fruitfulness is part of the proof that you are anchored to Jesus and persevering in the faith.

In this chapter, there is no encouragement for those whose lack of fruit shows a lack of faith. They are 'worthless . . . in danger of being cursed' (verse 8). The impossibility of their salvation is the judgment of God on their rebellion. By profiling these people, the author of Hebrews is giving us an important lesson. Their lack of progress is meant to be the spur we need to progress. Their danger of being cursed is meant to be the impetus that keeps us walking on the path to blessing. Their worthless fruit is meant to push us on to useful fruit.

God knows we are complex. He knows that on the journey of the Christian life we don't just need hope; we need warning. We don't just need good examples to follow; we need bad mistakes to learn from. We don't just need encouragement; we need fear. We need a carrot and a stick.

The point of reading about these people is not to make you doubt your salvation, but to make you diligent in your salvation. Because, as a pastor, the writer is not doubting them (verse 9). He is convinced they are saved because of their fruit. He has seen their work for the gospel, their love for the God of the gospel and how they helped the people of the gospel. And not just in the past; look at verse 10: 'you . . . continue to help them'. Genuine Christianity is never simply past tense. It's always present tense, always faithful to Christ today, trusting in Christ today. And the writer urges them to do this diligently until 'the very end' (verse 11).

Unbelievers need to know that religious works do not bring about eternal life, but believers need to know that religious works are a sign we are alive. Your faith in the gospel will always result in gospel fruit, which is why it is one of the grounds of the assurance of faith.

Are you producing fruit (John 15:5)? What is the evidence of your love for Christ? One proof is your diligence as a believer. It is stunning that the pastor to the Hebrews talks about laziness (verses 11–12). This church is being battered by persecution, and yet he sees one of the greatest threats to their persevering in the Christian life not in someone putting a knife to their throats and telling them to renounce Christ, but in the inclination of their hearts towards laziness. Don't give in to laziness! Put your faith into action today.

Day 16

Read Hebrews 6:1–20
Key verses: Hebrews 6:13, 17

....

¹³When God made his promise to Abraham, since there was no one greater for him to swear by, he swore by himself . . . ¹⁷Because God wanted to make the unchanging nature of his purpose very clear to the heirs of what was promised, he confirmed it with an oath.

We are not always good at keeping our promises, but God is. In verse 13, God throws down a promise built upon an unchangeable purpose (verse 17), and on top of that he builds an oath on the impossibility of him telling a lie. So what you have in Hebrews 6 is an oath on top of promise. Unchangeable purpose on top of unchangeable promise. A word that cannot fail on top of a word that cannot lie. And all of that built upon the unchanging, eternal character of God. Which means what? It's a promise you can bank everything on!

It was a promise Abraham did bank everything on. God had promised Abraham numerous descendants who would all come through Isaac. But hot on the heels of that promise, God tells him to sacrifice Isaac. How could Abraham kill not only his only son, but also the son of the promise? But Abraham is so confident in the promise of God that he would kill the child, knowing for certain that God would raise the child to keep the promise.

Let's put that in New Testament language: Abraham believes in resurrection. He knows that even if he were to sacrifice his son, God would raise him up. Faith, for Abraham, is not spread betting, it's not eggs in different baskets, it's all in. He raises a knife to kill his son. Why? He reasons that God can cause a resurrection. Some would call it risky or irrational. God calls it faith. Faith is a trust, a belief, in the promise of God – even in the face of death, and even when the only way out is resurrection.

We too can have faith in God's promises. Our salvation is as safe as Isaac's was when he was bound on the altar; not even death could finish him. That doesn't rule out suffering, but it guarantees hope. It doesn't rule out waves, but it promises an anchor. It doesn't rule out death, but it promises resurrection. The cross and the resurrection of Jesus are the proof that any promise God has ever made he keeps. Not even death can unearth the anchor of Christian salvation.

We can persevere during the darkest days because:

> no matter how many promises God has made, they are 'Yes' in Christ. And so through him the 'Amen' is spoken by us to the glory of God . . . God . . . makes both us and you stand firm in Christ. He anointed us, set his seal of ownership on us, and put his Spirit in our hearts as a deposit, guaranteeing what is to come.
> (2 Corinthians 1:20–22)

Day 17

Read Hebrews 6:1–20
Key verses: Hebrews 6:18–20

....

¹⁸God did this so that, by two unchangeable things in which it is impossible for God to lie, we who have fled to take hold of the hope set before us may be greatly encouraged. ¹⁹We have this hope as an anchor for the soul, firm and secure. It enters the inner sanctuary behind the curtain, ²⁰where our forerunner, Jesus, has entered on our behalf. He has become a high priest for ever, in the order of Melchizedek.

What does it mean to be a Christian? Verse 18 gives us a fascinating definition: someone who has fled to hope. Do you remember what your life was like before you were a Christian? Hebrews 9:27 explains you were destined to die and after that face judgment. That was my destiny, my life: I was hopeless. And when God's Word opened my eyes to my destiny, what did I have to do? I fled to

Christ. Becoming a Christian is not a lifestyle choice. It's a life-or-death choice. Fleeing to Jesus is not like travelling to a holiday destination; it's like a Syrian refugee fleeing a war zone, knowing the only alternative is death.

So you flee to Christ. Why? Because on the cross, he takes your destiny of death and judgment and he bears it as his own. You flee to the one who dies your death, who takes the judgment of God on your behalf. He tears the temple curtain in two to show that you are no longer barred from the presence of God, but instead welcomed in. The curtain is torn; the job is done – he has achieved your salvation (see Day 11). And he has not just achieved your salvation, he has also anchored it: 'We have this hope as an anchor for the soul, firm and secure. It enters the inner sanctuary behind the curtain, where our forerunner, Jesus, has entered on our behalf' (verses 19–20).

As quickly as a Christian flees from hopelessness to hope, Jesus runs from the cross to heaven to anchor that hope. Jesus not only achieves our salvation, but he also anchors it in the presence of God, and there he sits to pray you home. Your salvation is anchored in the eternal presence of God – the place where there are no storms, no shame, no suffering and no sin. It's safe and it's secure.

You may be acutely aware of the storms of suffering and the storms of your own sin. But while you are in the storm, you have not only a high priest who died on your behalf at Calvary, but one who is also interceding for you in heaven. Can the cross be undone? Can the curtain be stitched back together again? No. It's anchored in the continuing priestly work of Christ. That is an anchor firm and secure, hope for your soul.

> We have an anchor that keeps the soul
> steadfast and sure while the billows roll;
> fastened to the Rock which cannot move,
> grounded firm and deep in the Saviour's love!
> (Priscilla J. Owens, 'We Have an Anchor That Keeps the Soul', 1882)

Day 18

Read Hebrews 12:1–17
Key verse: Hebrews 12:1

. . . .

> [1] *Therefore, since we are surrounded by such a great cloud of witnesses, let us throw off everything that hinders and the sin that so easily entangles. And let us run with perseverance the race marked out for us.*

The Christian life is never described as a stroll in the park or a jog around the block. One metaphor used in the New Testament is that of a race. In 1 Corinthians 9:24–26, Paul says, 'Do you not know that in a race all the runners run, but only one gets the prize? . . . Therefore, I do not run like someone running aimlessly; I do not fight like a boxer beating the air.' He talks about running the race with great commitment, vision and a sense of focus. In 2 Timothy 2:5, Paul talks about the athlete who will win the prize only because he has run according to the rules. And at the end of his life, he says, 'I have fought the good fight, I have finished the race, I have kept the faith' (2 Timothy 4:7).

When Paul, and the writer to the Hebrews, used this metaphor of athletics, people knew what they were talking about. They were familiar with the famous Isthmian Games in Corinth and the Ancient Olympics begun seven hundred years before Christ. But what made the author of Hebrews pick on this athletic contest to explain ordinary Christianity? The New Testament writers somehow saw that there were important similarities, but also differences, between the Christian life and an athletic contest.

The similarity was that both the professional athlete and the professing Christian had to subject themselves to extreme physical, emotional and psychological demands. Both had stringent requirements and both had to make enormous sacrifices because of these demands. The difference between the athlete and the Christian was that the reward, honour and glory were more tangible and obvious for the athlete. At the end of the race, he would receive the winner's crown. But in the case of the Christian, the reward was not obvious or tangible. The recipients of this letter could not see their rewards. And so the author had to write to encourage them to keep in mind that there *is* a reward and that it *will* be given.

How are you doing in the race? The finishing line is in sight. One day you will receive your reward and know that your sacrifice was worth it. Will you press on so that you can say with Paul,

I have fought the good fight, I have finished the race, I have kept the faith. Now there is in store for me the crown of righteousness, which the Lord, the righteous Judge, will award to me on that day – and not only to me, but also to all who have longed for his appearing. (2 Timothy 4:7–8)

Day 19

Read Hebrews 12:1–17
Key verse: Hebrews 12:1

· ·

¹Therefore, since we are surrounded by such a great cloud of witnesses, let us throw off everything that hinders and the sin that so easily entangles. And let us run with perseverance the race marked out for us.

Are you beginning to flag and lose courage in the Christian race? The writer to the Hebrews urges us, 'Therefore, since we are surrounded by such a great cloud of witnesses . . . let us run with perseverance.' The 'therefore' causes us to look back to chapter 11 where we find the 'hall of fame' of the biblical world. The writer provides this long list of heroes of faith to inspire our own faith and to bolster our perseverance.

Over thirty-eight verses, the author patiently and persistently reminds his readers of story after story from the Old Testament. In fact, he mentions seventeen heroes by name, from Abel all the way to David. In addition, he talks about a few whole generations. A total of eighteen times in the Greek text of this chapter we read that the Christian race is to be run 'by faith'. You do not see the reward; you will not hold on to it; you will not have it as a tangible reality right now, so you need to have the ability to go 'by faith'.

Why does the writer go through such a lengthy commentary? He takes us back to the first human family, beginning with Abel, to underline that from the beginning of the human race until now, all our transactions with God have depended on the currency of faith. Faith is not something that began with the nation of Israel. We also learn that faith is not the gross simplification of the 'name-it-and-claim-it' religion that sometimes passes for Christianity today. Some Old Testament believers received tangible rewards in their lifetimes; others saw only the price of their faith as they experienced humiliation and even death (see Hebrews 11:32–40). But they were 'all commended for their faith' (verse 39). And faith, says Hebrews 11:6, is believing that God exists and that he's a rewarder of those who earnestly seek him. That's what chapter 11 records that these heroes of the faith did. What an inspiring example they set for us today!

Over the last two thousand years, our cloud of witnesses has expanded. We now have millions in the stadium watching us run the race. Imagine the ones who are personally cheering you on and calling out your name. It could be your Sunday school teacher, youth leader, parents or grandparents – those faithful Christians who prayed for you, explained and modelled the gospel for you, and have now taken their seats in the stadium to watch you run. Thank God for this cloud of witnesses. Today, let their testimony and encouragement inspire you to keep running your race with courage and perseverance.

Day 20

Read Hebrews 12:1–17
Key verse: Hebrews 12:1

....

¹Therefore, since we are surrounded by such a great cloud of witnesses, let us throw off everything that hinders and the sin that so easily entangles. And let us run with perseverance the race marked out for us.

What is holding you back from running the Christian race? The author says in verse 1, 'Let us throw off everything that hinders and the sin that so easily entangles.' He is thinking of certain factors that can impede our progress and compromise our good intentions. He distinguishes between weights and sins, and both need to be thrown off.

For too long, Christians have focused only on right and wrong. We say that as long as what I am doing is not wrong, it is OK for me. But God wants us to go beyond that legalistic mentality. The apostle Paul's argument was that if what I do is a stumbling block to my brother –

even though I have no conscience problem with it because it is not in itself a sin – still I will not do it for the sake of my brother (1 Corinthians 8). I am not simply asking, 'Is this right or wrong?' I am asking, 'Is this good; is this the best thing I can do?' Paul's point is that while something is permissible, it may not be beneficial.

The professional swimmer understands it is permissible to have long hair, but most male swimmers prefer to shave all the hair off their bodies! They want to ensure there is not a single weight that will add unnecessarily to the burden of their race. Athletes wear light clothes and shoes because they want to throw off every weight to ensure they have the best chance at the race.

But we don't only throw off the weights; we also throw off the sins. The author talks about 'the sin which so easily ensnares us' (NKJV). We recognize that sin can become our great obsession if we give it room. So don't nurture it, don't caress it, don't hide it. Simply throw it off and get rid of it. Jesus said that if your hand causes you to sin, cut it off (Matthew 5:30)! He is using hyperbole, but he is making a very important point: if your hand, which is so important to you, causes you to sin, do without it. Take radical and extreme steps to throw off sin from your life.

Friendship with a gossip, watching pornography, pride in your career . . . what sin do you need to stop nurturing and to get rid of? What weights – which relationships, priorities or activities, permissible but not necessarily the best choice – do you need to throw off if you want to make progress as a Christian? Take action today so that you can keep running your race with perseverance.

Day 21

Read Hebrews 12:1–17
Key verses: Hebrews 12:1–3

. . . .

> ¹*Let us run with perseverance the race marked out for us,* ²*fixing our eyes on Jesus, the pioneer and perfecter of faith. For the joy that was set before him he endured the cross, scorning its shame, and sat down at the right hand of the throne of God.* ³*Consider him who endured such opposition from sinners, so that you will not grow weary and lose heart.*

While the cloud of witnesses inspires us, our eyes are not fixed on them. We don't look at Abraham, Moses or David, great as they are. We don't look at Rachel, Rebekah, Ruth or Hannah, great as they are. We fix our eyes on Jesus, because *he* is our example. The example of Jesus instructs us. Built into the definition of Christian discipleship is the idea of imitating Jesus. In his first letter, John says, 'Whoever claims to live in him must live as

Jesus did' (1 John 2:6). Our claim to be disciples of Jesus must be matched by lives that emulate him.

When Jesus called people to become his followers, he called them with these words: 'follow me'. It didn't simply mean 'physically come after me', but 'learn to pattern your life after what you see in me'. And so Paul would later write, 'Imitate me' – mimic me – 'just as I imitate Christ' (1 Corinthians 11:1, NLT). Because after Jesus had ascended into heaven, the only way the early church could know how Jesus had lived was to look at the apostles, pastors and leaders who were imitating Christ and through them understand how to follow Christ.

It is important to learn to pattern our lives after Jesus, but here the author specifically wants us to look carefully at the way Jesus ran his race. His race, of course, was unimaginably demanding because it involved a Roman crucifixion, which was the most cruel and painful form of execution that had been devised. It was the most shameful way to be executed, since the victim was crucified naked after suffering terrible tortures. How did Jesus bear such humiliation and degradation? How was he able to endure such agony and shame? The author says, 'For the joy that was set before him he endured the cross, scorning its shame' (verse 2).

Amy Carmichael, whom we met in the introduction, suffered much over the course of her fifty-five years in India, rescuing more than a thousand young girls from prostitution. During the last years of her life, she was an invalid, writing books and poems from her bed. She wrote 'No Scar?'

No wound? No scar?
Yet as the Master, shall his servant be,
and piercèd are the feet that follow me.
But thine are whole; can he have followed far
who hast no wound nor scar?
(Amy Carmichael, *Toward Jerusalem*, Triangle, 1987, p. 85)

Suffering for being a Christian is part of what it means to follow Jesus. But *how* are you suffering? Are you imitating his endurance and single-minded obedience to God's purpose? Is the joy of future glory spurring you on?

Day 22

Read Hebrews 12:1–17
Key verse: Hebrews 12:7

....

> [7] *Endure hardship as discipline; God is treating you as his children. For what children are not disciplined by their father?*

'Everyone who wants to live a godly life in Christ Jesus *will* be persecuted,' writes the apostle Paul (2 Timothy 3:12, emphasis added). Not 'maybe' or 'probably', but everyone who wants to live a godly life in Christ Jesus 'will' be persecuted, which means you and me. You will suffer in some form or other, whether it's psychologically, mentally, emotionally or physically.

In this first-century church, there has not yet been a martyr (Hebrews 12:4), but still these believers are extremely discouraged. As they suffer for being Christians, the author will reinterpret their Christian experience of suffering. And the word he will use for that is 'discipline'. In the New Testament, the word for 'discipline' occurs twenty-one times, eight of them in this short passage. The writer talks about these disciplines that God has brought into our lives. In verses 5 and 6 he quotes Proverbs 3:11–12. He wants us to see our suffering for the sake of the gospel as God's discipline. Like a father disciplining his children, it is an experience intended for our benefit and not for our harm.

In our own situations, we need to learn to stand before God and say, 'God, I want to endure this hardship as discipline, as a training, as a means by which you are forming Christ more in me.' To this end, I have found the following poem – which spans the genders – a great encouragement. It is by an unknown writer.

When God wants to drill a man,
and thrill a man,
and skill a man,
when God wants to mould a man
to play the noblest part;
when he yearns with all his heart
to create so great and bold a man
that all the world shall be amazed,
watch his methods, watch his ways!
How he ruthlessly perfects
whom he royally elects!
How he hammers him and hurts him,

and with mighty blows converts him
into trial shapes of clay which
only God understands;
while his tortured heart is crying
and he lifts beseeching hands!
How he bends but never breaks
when his good he undertakes;
how he uses whom he chooses,
and with every purpose fuses him;
by every act induces him
to try his splendour out –
God knows what he's about.
(Author unknown; cited in J. Oswald Sanders, *Spiritual Leadership*, Moody Press, 1994, p. 151)

The Lord says, 'Those whom I love I rebuke and discipline. So be earnest and repent' (Revelation 3:19). Consider the hardships you are dealing with. What is God trying to teach you? What changes of attitude and behaviour do you need to make to be responsive, rather than resistant, to his discipline?

Day 23

Read Hebrews 12:1–17
Key verses: Hebrews 12:10–11

....

¹⁰God disciplines us for our good, in order that we may share in his holiness. ¹¹No discipline seems pleasant at the time, but painful. Later on, however, it produces a harvest of righteousness and peace for those who have been trained by it.

What are you looking forward to in your Christian life? As we run this race, the writer explains, there are rewards which, even now, we can receive. He outlines these rewards in verses 10–11. First, we begin to live holy lives, and second, we are drawn to a place of peace and righteousness.

God is holy, and those who live in Christ must live as holy people. 'Be holy, because I am holy,' says the Lord (1 Peter 1:16). He wants us to grow in our holiness so we may develop our friendship with him. 'Peace' suggests our relationships in society and in the church, that goodwill which grows as we learn to relate to one another. The writer says that as you go through this hardship, discipline and training, on the one hand, you will find yourself becoming more and more holy and walking closer with God; and on the other hand, you will find that your influence in the world will expand. In your family, your credibility will rise as you live faithfully, and as your credibility grows, your peace will grow, because the community that God has placed you in will begin to trust you and look to you more. Such credibility, however, will only result if we are willing to persevere, even in the face of misunderstanding and persecution (12:1–3). Often the faithful witness of an individual Christian, or the local Christian community, yields its fruit of credibility and peace only for the generation that follows. This is what makes persevering faith so crucial.

Now, in verses 14 to 17, the author reminds us that the race is a team effort. Of course, each one of us must make a strong personal effort to run our best race (verse 14). But don't think only of your race; think of other believers too (verses 15–16). Make sure you're looking out for those who need accountability and help. See to it that no one falls short of the grace of God. Never give up, and together let us run with perseverance the race that is marked out for us.

Be careful then, dear brothers and sisters. Make sure that your own hearts are not evil and unbelieving, turning you away from the living God. You must warn each other every day, while it is still 'today', so that none of you will be deceived by sin and hardened against God. For if we are faithful to the end, trusting God just as firmly as when we first believed, we will share in all that belongs to Christ.

(Hebrews 3:12–14, NLT)

Thank God for the Christian friends he has given you. Ask for his help as you hold each other accountable for living out the gospel. Pray for wisdom as you encourage your friends in the faith, share their struggles and help them recognize sin's hardening power. Speak Bible truth to each other, and spur one another on to finish the race well.

James and 1 Peter

A former vocal critic of Jesus and a friend who denied him may not seem the most likely people to offer wisdom on Christian perseverance. Or perhaps it was their experience of failure that actually made Jesus' brother James, and Peter, one of his closest disciples, ideal candidates to encourage beleaguered believers to keep on going.

James

Stephen's martyrdom in Jerusalem signalled a mass exodus, as believers fled throughout the Roman Empire. As leader of the Jerusalem church, what words of encouragement would James write to these persecuted believers? Perhaps, a little surprisingly, his key message was: faith works. Genuine belief inevitably transforms our speech, suffering, priorities and every other aspect of life. In just five chapters, James briefly touches upon a whole variety of issues that concern these new believers. He doesn't give an exhaustive treatise on any topic, but simply urges them to live out their faith, knowing that there is a value and purpose to their suffering.

1 Peter

The believers scattered through Asia Minor (modern-day Turkey) were not prepared for the persecution they were facing. Peter encouraged them to persevere by reminding them of God's eternal purposes, the example of Jesus' suffering and the privilege of belonging to God's people. The purpose of his letter was to give these pilgrims confidence in God's grace, whatever circumstances they faced: 'I have written to you briefly, encouraging you and testifying that this is the true grace of God. Stand fast in it' (1 Peter 5:12).

Day 24

Read James 1:1–8
Key verses: James 1:3–4

··

³You know that the testing of your faith produces perseverance. ⁴Let perseverance finish its work so that you may be mature and complete, not lacking anything.

Sometimes, remembering God has a purpose in allowing our trials helps us to endure them. In Romans 5:3–5, Paul teaches,

> We also glory in our sufferings, because we know that suffering produces perseverance; perseverance, character; and character, hope. And hope does not put us to shame, because God's love has been poured out into our hearts through the Holy Spirit, who has been given to us.

For both Paul and James, there is this great sense that perseverance is a productive area in which we grow, because trials test faith (verse 3).

We need to be prepared for trials. When difficulties arise, there is no point wondering, 'Why has this happened to me?' Just being a Christian does not mean you are never going to have any problems or illnesses. If so, becoming a Christian would save on health insurance! Living in our world means we will suffer – believers and unbelievers alike.

What matters is how we meet trials. We meet them 'God with us' – and also with the recognition that they test us not to break us, but to grow us and strengthen us. As Peter says,

> You may have had to suffer grief in all kinds of trials. These have come so that the proven genuineness of your faith – of greater worth than gold, which perishes even though refined by fire – may result in praise, glory and honour when Jesus Christ is revealed.
> (1 Peter 1:6–7)

Perseverance is not just putting up with these trials. It is an active, not a passive, word. It's courage and robustness. It's saying, 'All right – let's go for it!' This passage teaches that perseverance is us cooperating with God. James urges us, 'Let perseverance finish its work.' This means saying to God, 'Come on, Lord; I understand that this is a way in which you are moulding me to be more like Jesus.

I want to cooperate with you. Please grow me through this experience so that I become mature and complete.'

How are you coping with your trials? You can kick against them and blame God or you can persevere, cooperating with God's work. Will you grasp this trial as an opportunity to grow more like Christ? Will you view it as a means to get to know God better, pray more deeply and become more obedient?

In Christ's light, suffering is a ministry, not a millstone. It is a gift, not a glitch in the plan.
(Kristen Wetherell and Sarah Walton, *Hope When It Hurts: Biblical Reflections to Help You Grasp God's Purpose in Your Suffering*, The Good Book Company, 2017, p. 88)

Day 25

Read 1 Peter 4:12–17
Key verses: 1 Peter 4:12–13

. . . .

¹²Dear friends, do not be surprised at the fiery ordeal that has come on you to test you, as though something strange were happening to you. ¹³But rejoice inasmuch as you participate in the sufferings of Christ, so that you may be overjoyed when his glory is revealed.

Often suffering comes upon me as a surprise. And, in my default view, like many of us, I imagine, I'm looking and praying to get back to 'normal' as soon as possible. But these verses provide a radically countercultural perspective and a challenge to that default mode.

Peter explains that these trials are coming to test you. Your faith is more precious than gold; and gold is tested. It goes through fire, and then its purity is measured (1 Peter 1:6–7). It's not that you are stalked by a peril that's 'out to get you', but rather what is coming is to test you, and it is within God's plan and purpose.

In the midst of these trials, Paul calls us to 'rejoice'. I think the underlying meaning is: 'But *continue to* rejoice.' For me, rejoicing is gathering all the good things and being joyful about them. However, verse 13 says, 'But rejoice inasmuch as you participate in the sufferings of Christ.' How do we do that? It's not that we ignore the reality of sufferings, but that somehow we super-rejoice in the light of the future revelation of Jesus' glory: 'Rejoice inasmuch as you participate in the sufferings of Christ, so that you may be overjoyed when his glory is revealed.' So practise joy now, because we will be overjoyed then.

What Peter's saying here, from his own personal experience, is that fixing our eyes on the future helps us to face the present. How do you do that? You look back to the real Jesus of Nazareth, who died on the cross according to the Scriptures, and you look forward to his triumphant return. It's having our eyes trained not so much on the hardness of our circumstances, but on the foundation of the promises in Christ and the glorious revelation that is to come. It is the reality of what Jesus will do that is meant to flow back into our present – it breaks into our lives now, not removing our suffering, but helping us to live within it.

What are you praying for? It is not wrong to ask God to remove your suffering. But don't stop there. Try praying a bigger prayer – that if God does not choose to change your circumstances, he would use them to refine and prove your faith. Take encouragement from 1 Peter 1:3–9 as you consider the purpose of your trials and the future God has planned for you. Let the joy of Christ's return and the culmination of your salvation seep into your soul and have an impact on how you respond to your circumstances today.

Day 26

Read 1 Peter 5:1–11
Key verses: 1 Peter 5:8–9

....

>[8]*Be alert and of sober mind. Your enemy the devil prowls around like a roaring lion looking for someone to devour.* [9]*Resist him, standing firm in the faith, because you know that the family of believers throughout the world is undergoing the same kind of sufferings.*

The devil is not a box jellyfish, a deadly creature that floats through the sea and will sting you without thinking about it; you just drift into it. Our enemy, the devil, is not a stinging nettle that accidentally hurts you but has nothing against you personally. No! Our enemy is a 'roaring lion', a real, opposing enemy.

We're told to 'resist him, standing firm in the faith' (verse 9). This is not a call to aggressive spiritual warfare. Rather, as in Ephesians 6 and elsewhere in the New Testament, it is simply the call to stand faithfully for Jesus as his people – and to do so realizing that other Christians are going through the same thing.

Why is it important to realize that other Christians around the world are also suffering? Three reasons. First of all, it stops me seeing myself as a miserable exception. 'Woe is me! It's just me. The Lord is blessing all these other Christians and I'm the lousy exception.' Number two, it stops me seeing myself as a comfortable exception. 'Phew! I'm glad I live here and not there; I wouldn't like to go through that. I'll pray for them, but I'm glad it's not me.' Third, positively, I'm drawn into seeing myself as part of a worldwide fellowship. As believers, we're bound together as a whole, not just as a believing community but also as a suffering community. Remember Acts 14:22, the one bit of teaching for believers that's recorded in the book of Acts: 'We must go through many hardships to enter the kingdom of God.' This fellowship of suffering is about being brought to completion. And that's what Peter's saying here in verse 9.

Your suffering is not just an awkward little sting that accidently happened to you; it's personal. Be on your guard because the devil is prowling around, looking for someone to devour. Know that the same kinds of sufferings are being experienced by our brothers and sisters throughout the world, and it is part of God's purpose.

> This is . . . a life-or-death fight to the finish against the Devil and all his angels.
>
> Be prepared. You're up against far more than you can handle on your own. Take all the help you can get, every weapon God has issued, so that when it's all over but the shouting you'll still be on your feet. Truth, righteousness, peace, faith, and salvation are more than words. Learn how to apply them. You'll need them throughout your life. God's Word is an *indispensable* weapon. In the same way, prayer is essential in this ongoing warfare. Pray hard and long. Pray for your brothers and sisters. Keep your eyes open. Keep each other's spirits up so that no one falls behind or drops out.
>
> (Ephesians 6:12–18, MSG)

Day 27

Read 1 Peter 5:8–14
Key verse: 1 Peter 5:10

. . . .

¹⁰And the God of all grace, who called you to his eternal glory in Christ, after you have suffered a little while, will himself restore you and make you strong, firm and steadfast.

God knows what he is doing.

If God gives us decades to come, then that 'little while' of suffering may feel like an awfully long time. But in the span of God's things, if he would give us the eyes of faith, we'd see it as only 'a little while'. And in that little while, 'the God of all grace' – I think it is better translated as 'the God who produces and brings forth all grace' – has 'called you to his eternal glory in Christ'. He will comprehensively change things after you have suffered for a little while.

We're following in the footsteps of Jesus. The prophets looked to the 'sufferings of the Messiah and the glories that would follow' (1 Peter 1:10–11). We do not have a gospel of glory without suffering; we need to hold them both together. And we need to hold them in order: suffering for a little while, then glory to come for eternity.

Then what will this God of all grace do? He 'will himself restore, confirm, strengthen, and establish you' (verse 10, ESV). And it is 'you' plural. The spiritual house that's being built in your church fellowship, of which you are a living stone as you continue coming to Christ the living stone, might look shaky, but God will restore, confirm, strengthen and establish you (1 Peter 2:4–10). You are secure in Christ and in the purposes of God.

Peter concludes, 'I have written briefly to you, exhorting and declaring that this is the true grace of God. Stand firm in it' (verse 12, ESV). What is 'this'? 'This' is the message, the ethic, the worldview, the way of life in this letter. 'This' is the 'varied grace' (1 Peter 4:10) from God (5:10) that comes to us through Jesus (4:11). It's true, dependable grace, however beleaguered your Christian life might be. And variable grace trumps variable trials (see 1:6 and 4:10). 'This' is how things really are. The suffering that you face now or in the future for the faith is legitimate grace from God, not an awful mistake, not a tragic cul-de-sac; suffering for a little while, leading to glories to come – both bound up in grace. So stand fast, knowing it's for a little while, knowing that it's real, knowing that God's grace is even more real.

When faced with suffering, will you say to yourself, 'This is the true grace of God. [I will] Stand firm in it'? God will enable you to stand; his limitless grace is sufficient to match your current trial. Will you persevere, relying on his strength and believing his promise: 'My grace is sufficient for you, for my power is made perfect in weakness' (2 Corinthians 12:9)?

Revelation

As early as the end of the first century the future of the church hung in the balance. False teaching and internal division were rife. The Emperor Domitian had instigated another wave of persecution against those who would not worship him as Lord. The apostle John, exiled on the island of Patmos, wrote to encourage believers to resist the demands of the emperor, stand firm against the devil's schemes and look forward to Christ's triumphant return which would ensure their complete vindication. The book of Revelation is full of bizarre visions and is highly symbolic; it is written in an apocalyptic style. We won't understand every detail, but the message to resist compromising our faith and stand firm in trials comes across loud and clear.

Day 28

Read Revelation 22:8–21
Key verses: Revelation 22:8–9

. . . .

> *8I, John, am the one who heard and saw these things. And when I had heard and seen them, I fell down to worship at the feet of the angel who had been showing them to me. 9But he said to me, 'Don't do that! I am a fellow servant with you and with your fellow prophets and with all who keep the words of this scroll. Worship God!'*

The book of Revelation gives us a glimpse into the climax of history, the coronation of our Lord Jesus Christ. In 22:16, John gets to the end of this great revelation and explains its purpose by quoting the words of Christ: 'I, Jesus, have sent my angel to give you this testimony for the churches.' John realized that this revelation was for the church in every age and generation, so that we might be encouraged and strengthened knowing that history is heading towards an end point.

You can sense the anticipation (verse 20): 'He who testifies to these things says, "Yes, I am coming soon." Amen. Come, Lord Jesus.' We echo this, but in the meantime, in difficult church situations, at work where you are the only believer, how do you persevere?

The Bible warns us to avoid distraction. Did you notice that in verses 8–9 John falls down to worship at the feet of the angel who'd shown him the vision? It was such an amazing experience and he was so full of wonder that he fell at the angel's feet in worship. And the angel says, 'Don't do that! . . . Worship God!' (verse 9). The angel didn't want to be the focus of worship or the cause of distraction. Instead, he directed John to worship 'the Alpha and the Omega, the First and the Last, the Beginning and the End' (22:13).

In the same way, we need to make sure our focus is not in any sense captivated or sidetracked by the wrong things. It is possible to become distracted, even by good and godly things. We can be distracted about translations of the Bible, methods of church government and modes of baptism. We can major on minors, make mountains out of molehills and become distracted by the very things that are meant to lead us to love Jesus more and serve him better.

Jesus knows our perseverance in the faith gets tested when we're distracted, even by good things like Christian service. When we take our focus off Jesus, we tend to get anxious and stressed, and start to believe that our progress in the Christian life is all down to us. Look out for these tell-tale signs and be honest with yourself about what is distracting you. Relegate that distraction to its proper place and renew your allegiance to Christ. Through repentance, prayer and time in the Scriptures, get your focus back on him (Luke 10:41–42)!

Day 29

Read Revelation 22:8–21
Key verses: Revelation 22:14–15

. . . .

[14]Blessed are those who wash their robes, that they may have the right to the tree of life and may go through the gates into the city. [15]Outside are the dogs, those who practise magic arts, the sexually immoral, the murderers, the idolaters and everyone who loves and practises falsehood.

Jesus is coming back soon! So what are the things we should keep on doing, and what must we avoid? Jesus warns us in Revelation 22:14–15 to beware of dirt.

If we look back to Revelation 7:14, we read about those who have washed their robes and made them white in the blood of the Lamb. The tense in the Greek language denotes a once-and-for-all action. When you trust the Lord Jesus, your sins are forgiven; they are washed away by the blood of Jesus, shed on the cross; they are blotted out, and your name is entered into the Lamb's book of life. But here in Revelation 22:14, the word 'wash' is in the present tense: it is not to do with your salvation but that daily cleansing that you and I need. We need cleansing for that hasty word, for that unkind response and selfish attitude. This sense of the Lord Jesus' imminent return encourages us to keep short accounts with God and with one another.

Verse 15 provides a sharp contrast to the previous verse. In the Bible, the word 'dog' is a symbol of things that are impure and unclean. 'Outside' doesn't necessarily mean that sinners are sitting at the doors of the heavenly Jerusalem. Rather, the sense is that the unrighteous are not part of what goes on inside the heavenly city. The list of sinful practices is not exhaustive, but conveys the difference between righteous and unrighteous living. We are called to live clean in a dirty world.

We are not called to live self-righteously, with a holier-than-thou attitude, but to live righteously. To live as Jesus lived. He hung around drunkards, gluttons and the immoral, and they were attracted to him because he didn't write them off or look down on them. There was no element of self-righteousness that said, 'I am holy and you are inferior.' Rather, his righteousness was winsome and attractive. Jesus lived clean in a dirty world, and that is his call to each of us today.

Are you still coming to God for daily cleansing? Are you still passionate about dealing with the sin in your life? It is easy to become complacent and excuse sin. But Jesus' call is to press on, to persevere in the life-long pursuit of holiness (Romans 6:11–14; Colossians 3:1–10). Today, reflect on how much God hates sin. Ask him to stir your heart and renew your strength to say 'no' to sin and 'yes' to righteousness (Titus 2:12). Pray that your 'walk' would match your 'talk', and your life would attract people to Jesus and the gospel.

Day 30

Read Revelation 22:8–21
Key verses: Revelation 22:18–19

....

> ¹⁸*I warn everyone who hears the words of the prophecy of this scroll: if anyone adds anything to them, God will add to that person the plagues described in this scroll.* ¹⁹*And if anyone takes words away from this scroll of prophecy, God will take away from that person any share in the tree of life and in the Holy City, which are described in this scroll.*

What are the final words God wants to leave ringing in our ears as we press on in this life of faith?

First, there is a warning to watch out for deception (verses 18–19). This is a similar warning to the one the apostle John gave in 1 John 4:1–3:

> Dear friends, do not believe every spirit, but test the spirits to see whether they are from God, because many false prophets have gone out into the world. This is how

you can recognise the Spirit of God: every spirit that acknowledges that Jesus Christ has come in the flesh is from God, but every spirit that does not acknowledge Jesus is not from God. This is the spirit of the antichrist, which you have heard is coming and even now is already in the world.

John explains that many false prophets have gone out into the world, and in order to recognize, test and refute them, we have to know our Bible. We must have an intimate relationship with God – Father, Son and Spirit – through Scripture. We need to know our history and be familiar with the story of the church and what God has been doing in different generations and ages. We need to be people of maturity, like the men of Issachar who understood the times and knew what Israel should do (1 Chronicles 12:32).

But after the warning comes an encouragement. Look at the very last verse in the book of Revelation. Verse 21 is a wonderfully simple ending: 'The grace of the Lord Jesus be with God's people.' Today, whatever you face, God's grace is with you. God's grace is not something you have to stockpile at a Christian convention. Neither is it something you can leave behind at the end of an event. God's grace goes with you, and it is sufficient for everything that you face.

John Bunyan, author of *The Pilgrim's Progress*, taught,

> Grace can pardon our ungodliness and justify us with Christ's righteousness; it can put the Spirit of Jesus Christ within us; it can help us when we are down; it can heal us when we are wounded; it can multiply pardons, as we through frailty multiply transgressions.
>
> (John Bunyan, *The Riches of Bunyan: Selected from His Works*, ed. Taylor Anderson, CreateSpace Independent Publishing, 2017, p. 39)

Today, trust in God's grace to persevere, and live the life of faith well.

> May our Lord Jesus Christ himself and God our Father, who loved us and by his grace gave us eternal encouragement and good hope, encourage your hearts and strengthen you in every good deed and word.
>
> (2 Thessalonians 2:16–17)

For further study

If you would like to read more on the theme of perseverance you might find the following selection of books helpful:

- Christopher Ash, *Zeal without Burnout* (The Good Book Company, 2016).

- Dale Ralph Davis, *Slogging along on the Paths of Righteousness* (Christian Focus, 2016).

- Dale Ralph Davis, *The Way of the Righteous in the Muck of Life* (Christian Focus, 2016).

- Sharon James, *Ann Judson, A Missionary Life for Burma* (Evangelical Press, 2015).

- Paul Mallard, *Invest Your Disappointments* (IVP, 2018).

- Paul Mallard, *Staying Fresh* (IVP, 2015).

- John Piper, *The Roots of Endurance* (IVP, 2003).

- Helen Roseveare, *Digging Ditches* (Christian Focus, 2012).

Keswick Ministries

Our purpose

Keswick Ministries exists to inspire and equip Christians to love and live for Christ in his world.

God's purpose is to bring his blessing to all the nations of the world (Genesis 12:3). That promise of blessing, which touches every aspect of human life, is ultimately fulfilled through the life, death, resurrection, ascension and future return of Christ. All of the people of God are called to participate in his missionary purposes, wherever he may place them. The central vision of Keswick Ministries is to see the people of God equipped, inspired and refreshed to fulfil that calling, directed and guided by God's Word in the power of his Spirit, for the glory of his Son.

Our priorities

There are three fundamental priorities which shape all that we do as we look to serve the local church.

- *Hearing God's Word*: the Scriptures are the foundation for the church's life, growth and mission, and Keswick Ministries is committed to preach and teach God's

Word in a way that is faithful to Scripture and relevant to Christians of all ages and backgrounds.

- *Becoming like God's Son*: from its earliest days, the Keswick movement has encouraged Christians to live godly lives in the power of the Spirit, to grow in Christ-likeness and to live under his lordship in every area of life. This is God's will for his people in every culture and generation.

- *Serving God's mission*: the authentic response to God's Word is obedience to his mission, and the inevitable result of Christlikeness is sacrificial service. Keswick Ministries seeks to encourage committed discipleship in family life, work and society, and energetic engagement in the cause of world mission.

Our ministry

- *Keswick Convention.* The Convention attracts some 12,000 to 15,000 Christians from the UK and around the world to Keswick every summer. It provides Bible teaching for all ages, vibrant worship, a sense of unity across generations and denominations, and an inspirational call to serve Christ in the world. It caters for children of all ages and has a strong youth and young adult programme. And it all takes place in the beautiful

Lake District – a perfect setting for rest, recreation and refreshment.

- **Keswick fellowship.** For more than 140 years, the work of Keswick has had an impact on churches worldwide, not just through individuals being changed but also through Bible conventions that originate or draw their inspiration from the Keswick Convention. Today, there is a network of events that shares Keswick Ministries' priorities across the UK and in many parts of Europe, Asia, North America, Australia, Africa and the Caribbean. Keswick Ministries is committed to strengthen the network in the UK and beyond, through prayer, news and cooperative activity.

- **Keswick teaching and training.** Keswick Ministries is developing a range of inspiring, equipping, Bible-centred teaching and training that focuses on 'whole-of-life' discipleship. This builds on the same concern that started the Convention: that all Christians live godly lives in the power of the Spirit in all spheres of life in God's world. Some of the events focus on equipping. They are smaller and more intensive. Others focus on inspiring. Some are for pastors, others for those in other forms of church leadership, while many are for any Christian. All courses aim to see participants return home refreshed to serve.

- *Keswick resources.* Keswick Ministries produces a range of books, devotionals and study guides as well as digital resources to inspire and equip Christians to live for Christ. The printed resources focus on the core foundations of Christian life and mission and help Christians in their walk with Christ. The digital resources make teaching and sung worship from the Keswick Convention available in a variety of ways.

Our unity

The Keswick movement worldwide has adopted a key Pauline statement to describe its gospel inclusivity: 'all one in Christ Jesus' (Galatians 3:28). Keswick Ministries works with evangelicals from a wide variety of church backgrounds, on the understanding that they share a commitment to the essential truths of the Christian faith as set out in our statement of belief.

Our contact details

T: 01768 780075
E: info@keswickministries.org
W: www.keswickministries.org
Mail: Keswick Ministries, Rawnsley Centre, Main Street, Keswick, Cumbria, CA12 5NP, England

Related titles from IVP

Food for the Journey

The Food for the Journey series offers daily devotionals from well-loved Bible teachers at the Keswick Convention in an ideal pocket-sized format – to accompany you wherever you go.

Available in the series

1 Thessalonians
Alec Motyer with
Elizabeth McQuoid
978 1 78359 439 9

2 Timothy
Michael Baughen with
Elizabeth McQuoid
978 1 78359 438 2

Colossians
Steve Brady with
Elizabeth McQuoid
978 1 78359 722 2

Ezekiel
Liam Goligher with
Elizabeth McQuoid
978 1 78359 603 4

Habakkuk
Jonathan Lamb with
Elizabeth McQuoid
978 1 78359 652 2

Hebrews
Charles Price with
Elizabeth McQuoid
978 1 78359 611 9

James
Stuart Briscoe with
Elizabeth McQuoid
978 1 78359 523 5

John 14 – 17
Simon Manchester with
Elizabeth McQuoid
978 1 78359 495 5

Available from your local Christian bookshop or **www.ivpbooks.com**

Food for the Journey

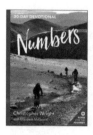

Numbers

Christopher Wright
with Elizabeth
McQuoid
978 1 78359 720 8

Revelation 1 – 3

Paul Mallard with
Elizabeth McQuoid
978 1 78359 712 3

Romans 5 – 8

John Stott with
Elizabeth McQuoid
978 1 78359 718 5

Ruth

Alistair Begg with
Elizabeth McQuoid
978 1 78359 525 9

Praise for the series

'This devotional series is biblically rich, theologically deep and full of wisdom . . . I recommend it highly.' **Becky Manley Pippert, speaker, author of** *Out of the Saltshaker and into the World* **and creator of the Live/Grow/ Know course and series of books**

'These devotional guides are excellent tools.' **John Risbridger, Minister and Team Leader, Above Bar Church, Southampton**

'These bite-sized banquets . . . reveal our loving Father weaving the loose and messy ends of our everyday lives into his beautiful, eternal purposes in Christ.' **Derek Burnside, Principal, Capernwray Bible School**

'I would highly recommend this series of 30-day devotional books to anyone seeking a tool that will help [him or her] to gain a greater love of scripture, or just simply . . . to do something out of devotion. Whatever your motivation, these little books are a must-read.' **Claud Jackson,** *Youthwork* **Magazine**

Related teaching CD and DVD packs

1 Thessalonians
SWP2203D (5-CD pack)

2 Timothy
SWP2202D (4-CD pack)

Colossians
SWP2318D (4-CD pack)

Ezekiel
SWP2263D (5-CD pack)

Habakkuk
SWP2299D (5-CD pack)

Hebrews
SWP2281D (5-CD pack)

James
SWP2239D (4-CD pack)

John 14 – 17
SWP2238D (5-CD pack)

Numbers
SWP2317D (5-CD pack)

Revelation
SWP2300D (5-CD pack)

Romans 5 – 8
SWP2316D (4-CD pack)

Ruth
SWP2280D (5-CD pack)

Available from www.essentialchristian.com

Related teaching CD and DVD packs

DVD PACKS

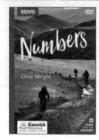

Colossians
SWP2318A (4-DVD pack)

Ezekiel
SWP2263A (5-DVD pack)

Habakkuk
SWP2299A (5-DVD pack)

John 14 – 17
SWP2238A (5-DVD pack)

Numbers
SWP2317A (5-DVD pack)

Revelation
SWP2300A (5-DVD pack)

Ruth
SWP2280A (5-DVD pack)